Community Cultures

Looking at Data

Leigh McClure

COMPUTER SCIENCE For the REAL World™

Rosen Classroom™

Published in 2018 by The Rosen Publishing Group, Inc.
29 East 21st Street, New York, NY 10010

Book Design: Jennifer Ryder-Talbot
Editor: Caitie McAneney

Photo Credits: Cover, 4 Rawpixel.com/Shutterstock.com; p. 6, 10, 12, 14 Africa Studio/Shutterstock.com; p. 8 Jamie Hooper/Shutterstock.com.

ISBN: 9781538351949
6-pack ISBN: 9781508136668

Manufactured in the United States of America

CPSIA Compliance Information: Batch #WS18RC: For Further Information contact Rosen Publishing, New York, New York at 1-800-237-9932

Table of Contents

My Community

There are many cultures in the world. Cultures are the ways of life of a certain group of people. America is home to many cultures. My community has many cultures, too. What can I learn about community cultures by looking at data?

A Project

First, I need to gather data. I use my computer to type a note about my **project**. I add a question at the end: "What is your family's culture?" Many people have more than one culture or **heritage**. I ask them to choose one.

Different Cultures

I print out the notes. I give them to people in my neighborhood. Then, I **collect** them the next day. Many people took part in my project! I count five cultures: Polish, American Indian, German, African American, and Puerto Rican.

Making a Chart

I make a chart with my data. I put a mark for each family with a certain culture. Five families have Polish heritage. Four families have American Indian heritage. Two families have German heritage. Three families have African American heritage. Six families have Puerto Rican heritage.

Polish	IIIII
American Indian	IIII
German	II
African American	III
Puerto Rican	IIIIII

What Does Data Tell Me?

I look at my chart. I see the most marks for the Puerto Rican culture. I see the fewest marks for the German culture. What else can I tell from looking at my chart? I know that there are more Polish households than African American households.

Polish	IIIII
American Indian	IIII
German	II
African American	III
Puerto Rican	IIIIII

Learning from Data

I make a pie chart and bar graph to look at my data in a different way. I learn a lot from looking at my data. Above all, I learn that there's a lot of **diversity** in my community!

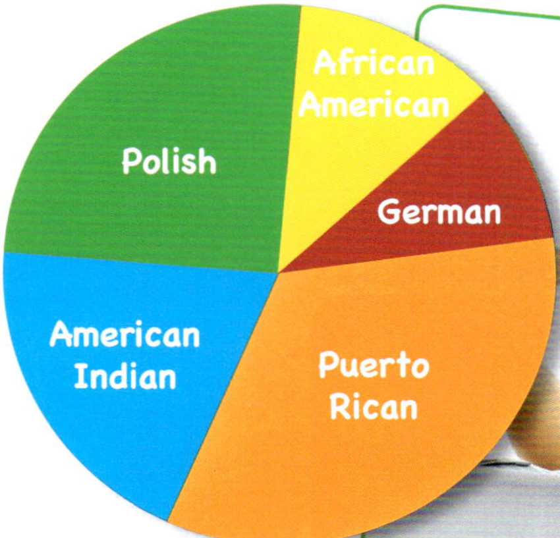

Glossary

collect: To gather together.

diversity: The state of having many things that are different.

heritage: Something that comes from past members of a family or group.

project: A task.

Index